W9-BSQ-612

TEXT AND PHOTOGRAPHY BY
ANNIE JENSEN

ADDITIONAL PHOTOGRAPHS BY
LAUREN ELIZABETH THORP
TIFFANY R. C. ROACH
JENNA M. THORP
CHRISTOPHER A. MOYER

A HEART FOR AFRICA

ROSEMARY JENSEN AND THE STORY OF RAFIKI

Kregel
Publications

A Heart for Africa: Rosemary Jensen and the Story of Rafiki

© 2007 by Annie Jensen

Published by Kregel Publications, a division of Kregel, Inc., P.O. Box 2607, Grand Rapids, MI 49501.

Scripture quotations are from the *Holy Bible, New International Version*®. Copyright © 1973, 1978, 1984 by International Bible Society. Used by permission of Zondervan. All rights reserved.

The front cover photo, *A Heart for Africa*, and the title page photo, *The Gate*, are by Annie Jensen.

Library of Congress Cataloging-in-Publication Data
Jensen, Annie
   A heart for Africa: Rosemary Jensen and the story of Rafiki / by Annie Jensen.
     p. cm.
   1. Church work with children—Africa. 2. Church work with teenagers—Africa. 3. Missions—Africa. 4. Rafiki Foundation. 5. Jensen, Rosemary. 6. Orphanages—Africa. I. Title.
BV2616.T46 2007
266.0096—dc22   2006029013

ISBN: 978-0-8254-3889-9

Printed in China

07 08 09 10 11 / 5 4 3 2 1

CONTENTS

ACKNOWLEDGMENTS

For the beautiful children of Africa

I wish to thank all those involved with the Rafiki Foundation, both in America and in Africa, who helped make this book possible by their hospitality, generosity, and patience. I would like to acknowledge Karen Elliot, Susy Harbick, and Susan Kaminski for their help in tracking down the smallest details, and Rosemary Jensen for bringing this project to me. Special thanks to my fellow travelers, who made the trip to Kenya, Malawi, Tanzania, Ethiopia, Rwanda, and Uganda in April of 2005 unforgettable, and to all those who were there to welcome us into their homes and into the soul of Africa.

My thanks to Dennis Hillman, publisher of Kregel Publications, for his interest and support, and for graciously extending the deadline when Hurricane Ivan struck my home and community. My appreciation to the staff at Kregel for their assistance with editing and artistic direction.

I am also grateful to Whitney Thorp, Kathy Cook, Tova Kreps, Dee Alford, Joyce McGee, and Brandy Holland for their friendship, unwavering support, and ongoing confidence in my ability to bring this book to completion while enmeshed in the process of rebuilding.

Finally, my deepest thanks to all those brave enough to open their hearts to interviews, and their faces and lives to the camera. I am especially indebted to the photographers whose art form graces these pages—Tiffany Roach, Lauren Thorp, Jenna Thorp, and Chris Moyer, as well as to Ryan Spencer, who filmed every interview for me.

The Curious Umbrella. Two girls by the roadside in Nigeria. (Lauren Elizabeth Thorp, 2004)

Sea of Children. Children from a nearby school crowd around to have their picture taken outside the Rafiki Girls' Center in Malawi. (Tiffany R. C. Roach, 2003)

INTRODUCTION

Rosemary Jensen

As you read the story of Rafiki, you'll be fascinated with what is happening in the lives of children in Africa. No doubt you are asking, "What is Rafiki?" Rafiki is one organization of ordinary people with a passion to help those less fortunate. *Rafiki* is the Swahili word for "friend," something greatly needed at this time in Africa. As a friend, Rafiki rescues orphans and vulnerable teenagers from death, disease, and poverty; declares the gospel of Jesus Christ to them; and educates them for productive living and leadership in their own countries.

When I was seventeen, I realized that God had given me a heart to be a missionary. Now, sixty years later, He has expanded that desire of my heart, taking it beyond me and involving many others in this ministry of mercy. In the early days of Rafiki, I had no great vision for an organization such as what exists today, and no one to guide me I simply did the next thing that God put before me, believing that He would lead me. He had already prepared me through college, teaching school, occupational therapy training in the military, and marriage to my doctor husband, Bob.

Two years after the birth of our first child we sailed out of New York Harbor for Africa as missionaries. That was the beginning of what has taken us many years to accomplish with so much yet to be done.

Many difficulties, discouragements, and pure hardships have been suffered in putting Rafiki together. But God has been faithful, and the work of Rafiki has expanded now into ten countries. Today, most endeavors aimed toward Africa attempt to change multitudes with mass programs. But Rafiki seeks others who might want to follow our lead in changing lives—one orphan at a time.

Why Rafiki at this time in history? I don't know all the reasons, but some are obvious. First, there are millions of orphans in Africa today. There are also millions of street-children, poor schools or no schools, unemployment rates of 60–80 percent, disease including AIDS, and in some places, starvation.

Another reason is that at perhaps no other time has there been a greater need for Christians to show gratitude to God for the grace and mercy He has shown us. Jesus said, "From everyone who has been given much, much will be demanded" (Luke 12:48).

Rafiki's work in Africa could, by God's grace, affect enough children's lives to change the whole continent. I cannot imagine what will result tomorrow from the work of Rafiki today, but we will continue to do the next thing He shows us to do. We trust that people like you, who care enough to read this book, will come alongside to help us accomplish God's plan for Africa to the praise of His glory.

Reflection. Birds in flight above pink flamingos in Ngorongoro Crater in Tanzania. (Annie Jensen, 2005)

1

THE GENESIS OF RAFIKI

In the Beginning . . .

Rafiki. In Swahili the word means "friend." With the intention of befriending those in need, Bob and Rosemary Jensen sailed to Africa in 1957 as missionaries, intending to work there the rest of their lives. Bob, a physician, sought funding to build a hospital in Moshi, Tanzania, and in 1964 the Kilimanjaro Christian Medical Center (KCMC) was founded. Rosemary, who first dedicated her life to cross-cultural missions at the age of seventeen, worked as a teacher.

The Jensens worked in Tanzania for the next nine years until their original plans changed and they returned to the United States in 1966.

Rosemary, who had been the executive director of the interdenominational Bible Study Fellowship (BSF) organization since 1980, first envisioned Rafiki as a sending agency that would establish BSF classes in Africa. In 1985, Rosemary sent two doctors and their families to Oshi to work at KCMC. Besides serving as medical staff, the two couples also worked for the benefit of the country and taught the Bible.

Contemplation. Bob and Rosemary Jensen relax in Bumbuli, Tanzania, their home during their first tour as missionaries. (from family photos, 1958–1961)

The Ritual. A young boy prepares for his entrance into adulthood in Tanzania. (Annie Jensen, 2005)

Kilimanjaro. The snow-capped Mount Kilimanjaro in Tanzania at the break of dawn. (Annie Jensen, 2005)

"Rafiki started because Bob and I lived out here," Rosemary explains. "We loved this place. That stayed in my heart all the time until we came back out."

In 1986, on the way back to the United States from a visit to Africa, Rosemary and Bob, along with her brother, Don McEachern, and their friend Richard Walenta, decided to form a foundation to help meet the needs of the people in Africa. They decided to call the foundation Rafiki. "It was a very overwhelming trip for me," Richard admits, remembering the great need he'd witnessed. "That was the first time I'd ever really been out of the United States."

By February 1987, the Rafiki Foundation was incorporated and officially registered as a 510c3, a nonprofit organization. Rosemary, Bob, Don, and Richard comprised its first board of directors. The Rafiki office was set up in the Jensen home, where Rosemary could organize the activities during evenings and weekends. She worked a dual role—executive director of BSF and general director of Rafiki—until her retirement from BSF in 2000, after which she devoted her full time to the foundation.

By 1992, because of the AIDS epidemic, Uganda alone was faced with the needs of 1.5 million orphans. Under Rosemary's direction, and in response to the crisis in Africa, the role of the Rafiki Foundation expanded from a sending organization to an organization that today endeavors to provide assistance to the whole person, including their physical, practical, educational, spiritual, and economic needs.

The Voyage. Rosemary and Bob Jensen and their first child embark from New York harbor on the *Oslofjord* in 1957 on their way to Africa. (from family photos, 1957)

Child Fishing. On Ghana Independence Day, the children at the Rafiki Children's Center choose an activity to do with their families. Kwasi, a child who was severely beaten in his home before coming to Rafiki, asks to go fishing. Shaking with excitement in anticipation, he saves his breakfast to use as bait. The rest of the world drops away as he baits his hook. (Tiffany R. C. Roach, 2003)

The Welcome. A woman waits beside the entrance of her home in the Ethiopian countryside to welcome guests. (Annie Jensen, 2005)

2

THREE ROPES

Rafiki's Lifeline to Ten Countries

Today Rafiki is legally registered in ten English-speaking African countries, and has acquired tracts of approximately fifty acres in or near towns in each country. There are operating Rafiki Villages in five of those countries, and the process is underway toward establishing villages in the remaining countries. The goal of Rafiki is to support the community by operating a home environment and schools for orphans, vocational schools for vulnerable teens, and free quarterly medical care for the surrounding area.

Each of the ten nations has its own history, climate, topography, languages, and people. What these countries share is the AIDS pandemic, which may be the greatest humanitarian crisis the world has ever faced.

According to UNICEF, the United Nations children's organization, while Africa accounts for only 12 percent of the world's population, it claims 43 percent of the world's child deaths, 70 percent of the cases of HIV/AIDS, and a staggering 90 percent of all children orphaned by AIDS. There are an estimated 43 million orphans in Sub-Saharan Africa, where 50 percent of the population lives on a per capita income of less than a dollar a day.

ETHIOPIA

With a population of 74.2 million (per UN, 2005), Ethiopia alone remained independent through the period of colonial rule of Africa. The country was occupied only briefly, by Italy between 1936 and 1941. Ethiopia's story in the past century, however, has been marked by violent strife and droughts. The agriculture-based economy continually suffers from insufficient water and poor cultivation practices. In addition, the government owns all land, making

Entrance. A typical home in rural areas of Ethiopia, as seen through the entrance of the woven twig wall surrounding the tiny enclave. (Annie Jensen, 2005)

Passengers. An Ethiopian man drives three women passengers to their destination in a horse-drawn carriage, a popular means of conveyance in Ethiopia. (Annie Jensen, 2005)

it impossible for entrepreneurs to use land as collateral for loans. As a result, growth in industry is hampered.

The average Ethiopian life expectancy is a mere forty-five-and-a-half years, owing partly to the 1.5 million HIV/AIDS-infected Ethiopians. In the early years of the twenty-first century, the orphan population reached 4.5 million (per UNICEF, 2005).

During 2005, land for an Ethiopian Rafiki Village was given to Rafiki by the government in Modjo.

GHANA

Ghana was the first independent nation formed out of the colonial system, when in 1957 the British Gold Coast merged with the Togo land trust. Ghana has a population of 21.8 million (per UN, 2005). The economy is supported by natural resources of gold, timber, and cocoa, and enjoys twice the per capita gross national product of other West African countries. Still, Ghana remains heavily dependent on international assistance. The domestic economy, which accounts for only 36 percent of the gross domestic product, employs 70 percent of the workforce.

The life expectancy of fifty-eight-and-a-half years is higher than in Ethiopia, but about three hundred fifty thousand people are infected with HIV/AIDS. One hundred seventy thousand were orphans shortly after the turn of the century (per UNICEF, 2003).

Rafiki missionaries have been working in Ghana since 1991, and the first Rafiki Village was dedicated in 2001 in Accra.

KENYA

Kenya has a population of 32.8 million (per UN, 2005). After independence from British rule in 1963, the government organized as a parliamentary democracy. Industries include small consumer goods, agricultural products, oil refining, cement manufacture, and tourism. Development has been hindered,

Fisher-boy. Kwasi walks along a path with his bamboo fishing pole in Ghana, West Africa. (Tiffany R. C. Roach, 2003)

though, by inefficient government control of important industries, pervasive corruption, and high population growth.

Life expectancy is forty-four-and-a-half years. About 1.2 million Kenyans live with HIV/AIDS, resulting in six hundred fifty thousand orphans (UNICEF, 2003).

Rafiki missionaries have served in Kenya since 1986, before the organization's official charter. A Rafiki Village in Nairobi was dedicated in 2004 on land donated by the Kenyatta family.

LIBERIA

Liberia has functioned under a transitional government since a 2003 agreement ended fourteen years of ethnic civil war. Over half of the 3.6 million people (per UN, 2005) are under age twenty. Although Liberia is rich in water, mineral resources, forests, and has a climate conducive to agriculture, the lack of security has impeded economic progress.

Over 11 percent of the people of Liberia are estimated to be infected with HIV/AIDS (per UN, 2004), although the war has made it impossible to determine the number affected. Liberia has thirty-six thousand orphans (per UNICEF, 2003), and life expectancy is now thought to be forty-seven-and-a-half years.

Rafiki received church-owned land for a village in Schiefflin in 2004.

MALAWI

Malawi became an independent nation in 1964 after being under British rule since 1891. The landlocked nation has a population of 12.6 million (per UN, 2005) and remains one of the world's least developed countries. Malawi's economy is dependent on other nations and in 2000 was approved for relief under the International Monetary Fund's Heavily Indebted Poor Countries Program. The economy is largely agricultural, and 90 percent of the Malawi people live in rural areas.

Malawi has one of the world's highest percentages of persons having AIDS,

Girl in Pink. A young girl pauses after running along Mombassa Beach in Kenya, East Africa. (Tiffany R. C. Roach, 2003)

Kibera. A jumble of rooftops sheltering some of the estimated 750,000 Kenyans living in the Kibera slums in Nairobi. (Annie Jensen, 2005)

Wash. Nigerian women do their laundry. (Lauren Elizabeth Thorp, 2004)

The Store. Two children purchase drinks at a store in Nigeria. (Lauren Elizabeth Thorp, 2004)

an estimated 1.1 million people in Malawi being infected with HIV/AIDS (per National AIDS Commission, 2003). Eighty-six thousand die every year from AIDS-related diseases, and life expectancy is thirty-eight-and-a-half years (per UN, 2003). In these early years of the twenty-first century, the number of orphans has reached a half million (per UNICEF, 2003).

A Rafiki Village was dedicated in Mzuzu in 2005.

NIGERIA

In West Africa, Nigeria operated for sixteen years under military rule until a peaceful transition to civilian government in 1999. With a population of 130.2 million (per UN, 2005), Nigeria is the world's sixth largest oil exporter. Cash crops include cocoa, palm oil, rubber, cotton, and peanuts.

In Nigeria, 3.6 million people are infected with HIV/AIDS, and orphans number 1.8 million (UNICEF, 2003). Nigerians have a life expectancy of fifty-one-and-a-half years.

Rafiki staff have been in Nigeria since 1990, and a Rafiki Village was dedicated in Jos in 2003.

RWANDA

Africa's most densely populated country, Rwanda's 8.6 million people (per UN, 2005) live in and subsist mostly by farming an area that is about the size of the state of Maryland in the United States. The tribal genocide since April of 1990, and particularly in 1994, caused massive population displacement. Extremist insurgency and two wars have discouraged international assistance and political reforms. The country struggles to right itself economically, even as it tries to foster reconciliation among embittered citizens. Ninety percent of Rwandans are involved in subsistence agriculture. Primary exports are coffee and tea.

Life expectancy in Rwanda is thirty-nine-and-a-half years, and the country has one hundred sixty thousand orphans. Two hundred fifty thousand people are infected with HIV/AIDS, including twenty-two thousand children under age sixteen (per UNAIDS, 2004).

Land for a Rafiki Village in Kigali was acquired in 2005.

TANZANIA

In 1964, following independence, Tanganyika and Zanzibar merged to form Tanzania. The first democratic elections in 1995 ended one-party rule of one of the poorest countries in the world. Although heavily dependent on agriculture, Tanzania's topography and climate limit cultivated crops to 4 percent of the land. Yet agriculture accounts for 80 percent of the workforce. The country offers little industry for its population of 38.4 million (per UN, 2005).

In a country in which the doctor/population ratio is 1/24,000 (per KCMC, 2005), life expectancy is forty-three years. About 2.2 million in Tanzania are infected with HIV/AIDS (per Global AIDS Program, 2003), and 1.5 million children are orphans (per GAP, 2001).

Rafiki missionaries have been in Tanzania since 1985, and land was provided by the church for a Rafiki Village in Moshi in 2005.

UGANDA

Uganda won independence from the United Kingdom in 1962, followed by nonparty presidential and legislative elections in the 1990s. Agriculture employs 80 percent of the 27.6 million people (per UN, 2005), with coffee the major export. Uganda is rich in natural resources, including fertile soils, regular rainfall, and sizeable deposits of copper and cobalt. Since 1986, the government has reformed the currency, raised prices on export crops and petroleum products, and improved civil service wages.

In spite of these reforms, the life expectancy in Uganda is only forty-six years. During the early 1990s, HIV/AIDS infections peaked at around 15 percent of the Ugandan population. By the end of 2003, the rate was about 4.1 percent (per UNAIDS), making Uganda one of the few African countries in which AIDS has

Genocide. Mass grave at the Kigali Memorial Museum is left open, as more bodies continue to be discovered every week —a result of the 1994 genocide in Rwanda. (Annie Jensen, 2005)

Tree Climbers. Two boys perch in a tree along the road to the Rafiki site in Rwanda. (Annie Jensen, 2005)

Bananas. A roadside market of green banana stalks in Uganda. (Annie Jensen, 2005)

actually declined. The estimated orphan population in 2003 was nine hundred forty thousand (UNICEF).

A Rafiki village was dedicated in Kampala in 2003.

ZAMBIA

Called Northern Rhodesia under British rule, Zambia took its new identity at independence in 1964. By 1991, elections ended one-party rule, but the government exhibited serious problems until an anti-corruption campaign was launched in 2002. Copper mining constitutes the largest industry in the country, and crops include corn, sorghum, rice, peanuts, sunflower seeds, tobacco, sugarcane, and cotton. The population of Zambia is 11 million (per UN, 2005), of which 70 percent live in poverty.

Life expectancy in Zambia is thirty-seven years, with an HIV/AIDS infection rate for the country of 16 percent (per U.S. Department of State, 2005). The number of orphans is estimated at six hundred thirty thousand (per UNICEF, 2003).

Rafiki acquired land from a church outside Lusaka in 2004.

Faced with statistics like these, the best efforts of the Rafiki Foundation can seem hopeless. But those involved with the organization remain undaunted.

Bob Jensen is often asked how he copes with having so few resources to tackle such immense suffering. He responds, "Would I stand back and say, 'I can't save them all?' No. I would save what I can. We must not be overwhelmed by our sorrow for so many, that we don't help the few we can. You save what you can, you reach out for even more, and you encourage others to do the same."

Or as Don McEachern responds, "If a hundred people were drowning in a river, and you only had three ropes, wouldn't you throw them?"

Hope. An evaporated watering hole under the blue sky of Ngorongoro Crater, Tanzania. (Jenna M. Thorp, 2005)

Tea Time. An African citril sips tea from an abandoned teacup at sunset high above Ngorongoro Crater, Tanzania. (Annie Jensen, 2005)

3

FIRST EFFORTS

Rafiki's Early Years

Rosemary Jensen went to Tanzania in 1988 to meet with the international division heads of Bible Study Fellowship (BSF). During that trip, she met with a long-time friend—Bishop Erasto Kweka of the Evangelical Lutheran Church in Tanzania (ELCT). When Rosemary asked Bishop Kweka what he saw as the greatest need in Tanzania, he said that his nation, especially the women, needed economic help.

To reach Tanzania, Rosemary had to travel through Kenya. She was struck by the differences between the two countries, particularly with regard to tourism. While Kenya was flush with items available for tourists to purchase, Tanzania's tourist market was negligible or even nonexistent. Inspired by her background in teaching and occupational therapy, Rosemary suggested to Bishop Kweka that Rafiki could send people out to teach these women how to make marketable products. The Bishop agreed to provide facilities and housing if Rosemary would provide the missionaries and a project for the vocational training of women.

That project was the beginning of the Rafiki Foundation's movement into areas other than medical care. Rosemary, with the help of her three adult daughters, developed a ceramic jewelry project that would provide goods marketable to Westerners. The four women experimented with the designs and the technical business skills needed, then instructed Rafiki missionaries in the techniques so they could train Africans.

Two couples were sent to Arusha to begin the project in a rehabilitation center run by the ELCT. The missionaries, whose work was funded by individual donations, began training local women to make and sell ceramic jewelry. The center in Arusha has flourished.

Bringing It Home. Children carry kindling wood up a hill in Tanzania. (Annie Jensen, 2005)

Curiosity. A woman in a traditional head wrap in Tanzania. (Annie Jensen, 2005)

Promised Land. A local woman and her child walk through the field designated for a Rafiki Children's Center. (Lauren Elizabeth Thorp, 2004)

As with Bob Jensen and Don McEachern, Rosemary did not let the overwhelming economic needs of the country discourage her. "One thing I learned fairly early," she says, "is to see the overwhelming needs, knowing I could not meet all those needs. . . . What you have to do is decide what it is that God has for you to do, and do that."

During the next two years, as the work of Rafiki expanded into Ghana, Kenya, Nigeria, and Uganda, it became increasingly difficult for Rosemary to direct the work of both BSF and the Rafiki Foundation.

In 1990, Dr. James Boice, an evangelical church leader and member of the BSF board, convinced his fellow board members that BSF should provide office space and staff to facilitate administration of Rafiki. The two organizations started sending out BSF-trained teachers, who volunteered their expertise in social work, dentistry, education, finance, and vocational training. Funding for these projects was provided by private donors, while BSF provided course materials and training.

Exhilarated by the expanding work of Rafiki, Rosemary organized a trip to Kenya, Tanzania, and Uganda in 1992. An invitation was extended to the BSF board members to join her and see the results of the two organizations' combined efforts. Rafiki staff also managed to arrange an audience with Janet Museveni, who was—and at this writing still is—the first lady of Uganda. Mrs. Museveni brought the group to Mausalita, an orphanage she founded, and asked Rosemary if Rafiki could help care for Uganda's 1.5 million AIDS orphans.

"She has a great heart for orphans," Rosemary recalls, "and for women in particular."

That night, as Rosemary and other members of the group looked out over the skyline of Kampala from their hotel room, she began to think about what Rafiki could do to assist the orphans.

By 1998, the success of the vocational training centers had led to similar Rafiki projects in Brazil, Ecuador, India, Madagascar, Mexico, South Africa, and Zimbabwe. All of these training centers were later closed to allow for a more concentrated focus on the English-speaking African countries in greatest need,

Market in Moshi. Carefully measured piles of grain and corn meal in the outdoor market in Moshi, Tanzania. (Tiffany R. C. Roach, 2003)

but before 2000, the Rafiki Foundation and BSF operated in twelve nations. As Rosemary neared the end of twenty years as executive director of BSF, the board asked what she would like to do if money were not a concern. Her answer was immediate—she would build an orphanage in Uganda. As a retirement gift to Rosemary, BSF gave enough money to Rafiki to make the first Rafiki Children's Center a possibility. Then another donor stepped forward to make that orphanage a reality, offering a generous gift—$1 million.

Mangoes. A heavily laden mango tree in Ethiopia in an area with irrigation. (Annie Jensen, 2005)

4

FOR THE LEAST OF THESE

Rafiki Orphanages Begin

With funds in hand, a search for land began in Uganda, as well as in Kenya, Nigeria, Tanzania, and Ghana. Ghana was the first country to locate and procure enough acreage for the first Rafiki Children's Center (RCC) in Africa.

Retired architect Chris Moyer donated time and expertise to develop a construction plan and blueprints for the Ghana Children's Center. The first phase of construction was to include a school building, a dining hall and kitchen, and six cottages. The plan was to accommodate ten children in each cottage, cared for by a native woman who would become the mother of those children.

Chris continues to work with Richard Walenta, who admits the biggest problem has been locating the right property—approximately fifty acres—for each Rafiki project. As land becomes available for Rafiki projects, the Foundation legally registers as a nongovernment organization. "We've acquired land from private individuals, from churches, and from the government," Richard says. "Land is precious out here to the people—they use every square inch. Property is always donated. We try to stay away from property with houses on it because we don't want to dislocate people. And we try to stay away from [paying] annual fees."

Development of the Rafiki building sites is a time-consuming process. According to Chris, "We want to see what land is available, get a survey of it, then I lay out the site plan. I might do two or three options. Once we have a completed site plan, we come back and have meetings with potential contractors. We usually build the infrastructure first—walls, bore holes, and roads."

Richard agrees. "It takes several trips to the site," he says, "before we actually begin the building process. We try to get out [to the site] at least once during the first phase of construction. We have the Rafiki Overseas Staff (ROS) person assigned to be our on-site representative deal with the contractor on a daily

Malawi Child. A young boy peers through the leaves of corn next to a site considered for a Rafiki Children's Center in Malawi. (Tiffany R. C. Roach, 2003)

Baby. A newborn Zebra in Ngorongoro Crater, Tanzania. (Annie Jensen, 2005)

Rwanda Road. The steep road to a potential Rafiki land site in Rwanda. (Annie Jensen, 2005)

Uganda Girl. A mother restrains her child from straying too far into the dusty street in Uganda. (Annie Jensen, 2005)

The Survey. From left, Ismael Amani, Richard Walenta, and Chris Moyer study the site survey for the Rwanda Rafiki Village as Ryan Spencer films the proceedings. (Annie Jensen, 2005)

basis." Because of the immediacy of e-mail and the availability of an on-site representative, Richard is able to oversee from America every phase of the building process.

"When I come to a site," Richard says, "I can see that site finished. And I can see the children. So that's a real goal of mine, to complete those buildings, so they can be occupied by children."

Construction on the property in Ghana began in early 2000. By June 2001, the first Rafiki Children's Center had opened its doors. In the meantime, Rafiki began acquiring land for children's centers in Nigeria and Uganda.

According to John Chun, an attorney who provides legal assistance to Rafiki, the process for procuring land in Nigeria was difficult, leading to many fruitless discussions. Another trip to the country was arranged.

"It was some time after 9-11," John recalls. "We went over there assuming

Malawi Baby. A young girl carries a baby on her back across the fields in Malawi. (Tiffany R. C. Roach, 2003)

Comfort. A girl keeps her young charge close by her side in rural Ethiopia. (Annie Jensen, 2005)

we would force the government in some way to acquire the land. When we got there, there was a 'big trouble' and a curfew from 7 p.m. to 7 a.m."

With this poor start, the attorney expected that he would accomplish nothing when he met with government representatives. But at the meeting, something remarkable happened; an official handed to him the deed to a beautiful piece of land. Nothing else was required.

In Nigeria, it wasn't until the dedication ceremony in 2003 that the story behind that land donation was revealed. The acreage had been given to Rafiki by Adamu Adiwu, the only son out of nine children. His father had been raised by missionaries, and through their efforts he had become a teacher and educated all nine of his children. Adamu later graduated from Harvard University and became an attorney. At his father's death, Adamu inherited the land. He had promised his father that he would someday help a Christian missions organization. He said he saw in Rafiki something of the spirit of the Christians who had come to Nigeria in the past to provide hospitals and schools.

In Uganda, Rafiki looked at nine pieces of property before finally choosing a site. The children's center in Uganda opened in February 2003.

With children's centers in Ghana, Nigeria, and Uganda, Rafiki redoubled its efforts in Kenya. Steve Kranz, who was part of the Rafiki Overseas Staff, met with Kristina Pratt, daughter of Jomo Kenyatta, who led the transition of British East Africa to Kenya and was for many years president. Would Kristina or anyone in her family donate land to the Rafiki Foundation? She smiled and responded, "Kenyans don't even give land to Kenyans, much less to *wazungu* [foreigners]." Rafiki spent months pursuing other leads until Kristina offered twenty-five acres of Kenyatta family land outside Nairobi.

"I could not stop thinking about our conversation," she explained to Steve. "I knew I had land that I was supposed to give. God would not give me peace until I did." Construction on the site began in mid 2002, and the fourth Rafiki Children's Center opened in January 2004. Kristina helped her mother, Mama Ngina Kenyatta, establish the Kenyatta Memorial Trust, which has extended the work of Rafiki in Kenya.

Cactus. A flowering cactus found on a potential Rafiki land site in Ethiopia. (Annie Jensen, 2005)

Matata ("trouble"). Two boys enjoy their time on the pier in Dar Es Salaam, Tanzania. (Tiffany R. C. Roach, 2003)

The first four Rafiki Children's Centers were secured, built, and dedicated in four years, ready to house some of the 12 million orphans scratching out an existence in sub-Sahara Africa—children who have been left behind, or as Bob Jensen calls them, "the least of these."*

"Every time I visit the places that took a lot of prayer and effort and funding," Rosemary says, "and I see it in reality, I'm overwhelmed with the grace of God and motivated to do more."

Serenity. A view of the Kenya Rafiki Village whose land was donated by the Kenyatta family. (Annie Jensen, 2005)

*Then the King will say to those on his right, "Come, you who are blessed by my Father; take your inheritance, the kingdom prepared for you since the creation of the world. For I was hungry and you gave me something to eat, I was thirsty and you gave me something to drink, I was a stranger and you invited me in, I needed clothes and you clothed me, I was sick and you looked after me, I was in prison and you came to visit me." Then the righteous will answer him, "Lord, when did we see you hungry and feed you, or thirsty and give you something to drink? When did we see you a stranger and invite you in, or needing clothes and clothe you? When did we see you sick or in prison and go to visit you?" The King will reply, "I tell you the truth, whatever you did for one of the least of these brothers of mine, you did for me." (Matthew 25:34–40)

Where the Goats Graze. The rocky hillside next to the Nigeria Rafiki Village. (Lauren Elizabeth Thorp, 2004)

5

FOUND

Stories of Orphans and Mothers

Afua was born on February 4, 2000. Weighing about four pounds, she was so small she could still be held in one hand when she was placed in a government orphanage by Ghana Social Welfare less than two weeks later. Her mother had been found roaming the streets and was taken to a mental hospital for treatment. Eventually, Afua was considered abandoned. A year-and-a-half later, she became the first orphan taken in by the first Rafiki Children's Center (RCC) in Africa.

Another child, Victory, came to the RCC in Jos, Nigeria, when she was sixteen months old. At thirteen pounds, she was one of the most malnourished children the physician working with Rafiki had ever seen. Three months after coming to the Center, she was able to stand on her tiny legs. Three months after that, she was running.

Atembem arrived with her younger brother and cousin at the Rafiki Children's Center in Ghana, two weeks before Christmas in 2001. At birth, her mother had given her a name meaning "I have nothing." She was abandoned by her mother and never knew her father. When her grandmother, who was unable to care for her, discovered that Atembem could live at the Rafiki Children's Center, she changed Atembem's name to Atarebono, which means "I have everything."

Barbara Anderson, the RCC director in Ghana, sent an update to Rafiki headquarters in April of 2005 about three other children who had been screened for admittance to the center. Barbara wrote,

> As you may recall, a man last year on his death bed wished his three small boys be placed in the custody of Rafiki—which he had heard about through Rafiki Mother Lizzy. However, when

Compassion. Mama Victoria, one of the mothers at home in the Nigeria Rafiki Village. (Lauren Elizabeth Thorp, 2004)

Lorine. Lorine waits patiently next to her assigned seat during school at Kenya Rafiki Village. (Jenna M. Thorp, 2005)

the man died (the mother had died earlier), the village elders denied the birth father's request and refused to cooperate with the children's uncle and social welfare. Instead, the village elders stole the boys from the uncle and placed the responsibilities to various families in their village. . . .

This past weekend during her leave, Mama Lizzy saw one of the boys and heard reports he was being abused. She saw that one of his hands [was] severely burned and asked the Christian uncle what had happened. She learned that as an "act of discipline" the boy's [hand was] placed in boiling water to teach him a lesson. This uncle said the elders [had] stripped away all his authority for the children a year ago and he had no control of the abuse happening to the children.

The first set of triplets was taken in by Rafiki after their mother died in childbirth. Another one-year-old was found by police, wandering abandoned on the street in the middle of the night. Many of the children taken in by Rafiki have been abandoned—some in pit latrines, others in taxi parks. Some have been left at the gate. Before entering a center, most have never slept in a bed or seen water running from a faucet. Many are malnourished and arrive with nothing except the clothes they're wearing. Others do not even have clothing.

In August 2004, Vivian Rogers, then director at the Kenya RCC, reported,

Today we brought home four-and-a-half-pound David. He is one month old. He shared a hospital bed with another infant, also abandoned. None of the children are clothed, diapered, or covered with a blanket. They sleep on plastic mattresses in a bed so small two newborns sleep up against each other.

Women wait in the room to feed the babies since there is some money in feeding the babies. The babies are fed at least until they fall asleep. Nobody keeps them awake if they eat less than an ounce of food.

Victory. A survivor of malnourishment, Victory is all smiles today. (Lauren Elizabeth Thorp, 2004)

When we arrived at the hospital they asked why we could not take more babies. There are now nine. I wanted to cry.

Holding one of these precious little ones is sweet. I consider the cost of him being in my arms. A mother who had no other choice. A woman who will wonder all her life where her baby went, if he lived at all.

David is so tiny. His new Rafiki mama named him David. The hospital named him Nursery Annex, where he was found.

Many of the Rafiki mothers have themselves been abandoned or widowed. Most are women with few prospects for making ends meet. The mothers must be Christians between thirty and fifty years old, literate in English, single, and in good health. Their own children must be grown and self-reliant. These women are placed in a home with a growing family of children who need them.

David's Rafiki mother is called Mama Lydia. She comes from a family of six children but was disowned by her Muslim parents when she converted to Christianity while in school. "Because I became a Christian," she says, "my family told me I can stay at the pastor's house. The pastor went back to talk with my parents, but I was turned away." The pastor's family took her in as one of their own.

"I became a missionary," Lydia says, "and was sent to Uganda, Tanzania, Rwanda, and Congo. When I was there preaching, I just forgot about my family. But I could not be moving with the pastor's family all the time." The pastor approached Rafiki about Lydia, and now she is mother to seven children.

Cottages accommodate as many as ten children, who are cared for by someone like Lydia or Ruth, who is also at Nairobi Rafiki Village. "When I came here I first began with four children," Ruth says. "Right now I have eight children." She smiles as she talks about one of them, Lorine, who arrived at the Center when she was five years old.

Lorine is a wonderful girl that God gave to me. When she first came here she was crying very much. She did not like to be held

The Dawn's Wash. Three children head for the campus laundry in the early morning light at the Nigeria Rafiki Village. (Lauren Elizabeth Thorp, 2004)

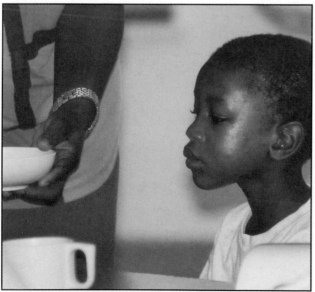

Christmas Breakfast. Timothy is served breakfast on Christmas Day in the dining hall of the Kenya Rafiki Village. (Tiffany R. C. Roach, 2003)

[by] anybody. She was not friendly. She was somehow *hard,* and I was wondering, *How am I going to stay with this child?* Because when she is messy, and I tell her "time out," she will not go. She was very difficult. She would scream. I would put her in time out, and she would throw a fit and tear things away, but God helped me to be patient with her, and I prayed to God to open her heart, and He gave me some words to say to her.

I cannot say now that she is perfect, but at least God has done a very, very, very great job in that child. I look at the way she began and the way she is now, and I think, *She is the best child.* I cannot say that I am a top mother, because I did not do anything, but when you depend upon the Lord, He is able to change the situation that we could not believe.

According to Rafiki Overseas Staff person (ROS), Becky Karschney, the Children's Center director in Kenya, Lorine was brought to the hospital for treatment when she was three years old. The adult who brought her never came back. Three months later, Lorine was assigned to a local children's home that struggles to care for too many children who have been misplaced, abandoned, or orphaned. "There are not enough workers, so they do not have a normal schedule. It is what I would call an unsupervised environment for far too many children—possibly over one-hundred-eighty children are in this facility. Lorine was very fearful and very angry when she first came to Rafiki. That's why she did not want to stay."

As Lorine grew to trust Mama Ruth, she began to talk about her past. Ruth says,

At first I thought that maybe she is just guessing. But I take time, and when we are sitting, she tells me again the same, same story. She told me that "my uncle took me to that children's home and in [that] home we were beaten by the [workers with] a cane

School Girl. Abigail and Atarebono wait for their day to begin at Ghana Rafiki Village's school. (Tiffany R. C. Roach, 2003)

Kenyetta House. The front view of the Africa branch office at Nairobi Rafiki Village in Kenya. Originally a vacation retreat, the three-story home was given by the Kenyatta family. The ground floor is used for meetings, conferences, and entertaining. The second floor has space for a missionary family and staff offices. Bob and Rosemary Jensen stay in the third-floor apartment when they are in Africa. (Tiffany R. C. Roach, 2003)

The Clothesline. Laundry too delicate for the dryers hangs on a clothesline at the Kenya Rafiki Village. (Jenna M. Thorp, 2005)

Front Step. Stephany, Brian, and Mary are entranced by the sound of a visitor's camera rewinding film outside their cottage in the Kenya Rafiki Village. (Jenna M. Thorp, 2005)

that can feel very painful." So I think that is why she was very fearful.

The other thing she told me is that "my mom died and somebody shoot her." I asked her why. "Because she burned me here." She has a scar on her cheek. Always she tells me, "It was my mom who burned me here." I have learned that she is a child who can keep the memories. She is very sharp. And so she may remember what happened at three.

All of the Rafiki mothers have "aunties" who come daily to help with cleaning the house and caring for the children. "We help each other," Ruth says. "We work together. When we [the house mothers] go out on our day off, they are there to remain with the children."

Ruth is also mother to Jimmy and Jane, twins who arrived at Rafiki when they were eighteen months old. "They could not walk," Ruth recalls. "They would just sit down. They were very tiny. They weighed nothing. And I was afraid because I thought they were not going to survive because they could not eat. They would only take porridge, and they did not like milk."

Becky explains more about Jimmy and Jane:

What I know about Jimmy and Jane is that they were taken to [a] baby home, and they were separated from the rest of the population because they had tuberculosis, and they were set naked on rubber sheets, or just a mattress, with bars all around them. But they were set in the same crib, which is what we think helped them to survive, because at least they had their own body touch with each other. But they were virtually [only] fed and cleaned up. The mattress would be cleaned, but they would be left alone. And these children were left in isolation for probably six months.

The first time we saw them we were debating—are they healthy enough? Would they survive? We were praying a lot about whether these children should come to Rafiki. Jimmy had started to curve in on himself. He could not sit straight. And he was so withdrawn. No eye contact. There was no joy. It was like looking at a dead baby, but he was still breathing. We were concerned about brain damage—what had happened because of their diet and isolation. And Jane was also very thin and very, very weak.

When we went back a month later to bring them to Rafiki, they had declined even further. So Ruth had her arms filled with these two babies who were totally dependent. They were acting developmentally as if they might have been six months old, but yet they were eighteen months old.

"Now as I see them walking and running around," Ruth says, "I thank God for that. Jimmy is now very strong. And he is very heavy. I cannot lift him. Jimmy was afraid. He didn't like strangers. But now he is getting free with everybody."

"We are seeing that God is the God of miracles," Becky says. "Just today when I stuck my head into the cottage, Jimmy said, 'Hi, Aunt Becky!' I thought, 'Wow!' Just a month ago, he would not have said my name. [Jimmy and Jane] are growing together, and this is in a period of under a year that we have seen this transformation happen, and it's God's grace."

"I have never been a mother before," Ruth says, "and having eight children—especially those who are not of your blood—it takes the hand of the Lord to love them and to accept them the way they are. But God had already prepared me for that, because throughout my life I had been loving to be with children, and I did not know why. I had been praying for God to give me strength, and understanding, and wisdom so that I may be able to manage these children. My call is to reach these children in the hand of God."

Story Time. Abena listens intently to a story during school at the Ghana Rafiki Village (Tiffany R. C. Roach, 2003)

Malawi Road. The road leading to the Malawi Rafiki Village. (Jenna M. Thorp, 2005)

Untitled. A small girl follows the team from Rafiki around the future Malawi Rafiki Village site. (Tiffany R. C. Roach, 2003)

6

GIRLS' CENTERS

Rafiki's Answer to Orphan Factories

At the dedication ceremony for the Rafiki Children's Center in Ghana in 2001, Mary Amadu, National Executive Director for the Department of Social Welfare in Ghana, was the keynote speaker. Her words introduced another dimension to the work of Rafiki: "We need to find some way to stop the orphan factories in the nations of Africa."

The "orphan factories" she referred to are the bodies of young girls who survive through prostitution. Add to their number the many women who were systematically raped during the wars in Rwanda and Liberia—numbers that are only now coming to light as women who have kept quiet all these years begin to seek medical help for advanced AIDS-related diseases.

AIDS has wreaked havoc on an entire generation. Young girls face abuse of relatives reluctant to take them in. Children take on the workload of an adult, live in unsafe conditions, and provide care for younger siblings. In Rwanda, more than eighty-five thousand families are headed by a child, usually a girl. The majority of these girls cannot afford to attend secondary school after completing government-sponsored primary school. With no hope of further education, little is left for these girls other than a life of poverty.

In response to Mary Amadu's urgent message, Rafiki sought to provide a way to meet the vocational and educational needs of these young girls. A prototype—training women in Arusha, Tanzania, in ceramic jewelry making—had been operating since 1988. From that prototype, the Rafiki Girls' Center (RGC) was born. At the center, girls are taught a core curriculum that addresses general vocational and life needs. They also receive specialized training in manufacture of a product. Each center produces its own kinds of wood carving, weavings,

Fuel. Neatly stacked fruits and vegetables, available for sale, adorn a gas pump in Nigeria. (Lauren Elizabeth Thorp, 2004)

A Girl. A young girl observes the festivities during the dedication of the Nigeria Rafiki Village. (Lauren Elizabeth Thorp, 2004)

baskets, painted crafts, and cloth accessories. To avoid competition with the local economy, these products are sold in America through the Rafiki Exchange in San Antonio and on the Rafiki Web site. The proceeds help meet the financial needs of the center.

Deb Nederhoed, who manages one of these centers, says, "For most of the students, school fees are the biggest obstacles. Many are orphaned. Others have lost one parent."

Girls aged thirteen to eighteen are admitted to the school. They pay no tuition and follow a three-year program of Bible, English, cooking and nutrition, health and hygiene, home and child care, sewing, business machines and computers, entrepreneurship and business administration, art and music, social graces, and citizenship. The staff consists of the center director, the director's assistant, production manager, designer, bookkeeper, laborers, guards, instructors, and teachers. The centers are nonresidential and can accommodate as many as sixty students. The teachers are volunteers and paid nationals.

In addition to the staff, buildings, and maintenance, the Rafiki Foundation provides one meal per day plus tea. In Malawi, that meal was, in fact, the girls' only meal; it was learned that the girls were eating grass to ease their hunger.

Often acceptance into the Rafiki Girls' Center means a girl will not have to "work at night" as a prostitute—but it is more than that. Most of the students have never held a paintbrush, drawn a picture, or played a musical instrument. When survival consumed their every thought, these girls could never even imagine expressing themselves in sculpting, weaving, sewing, and carving.

A typical day at each center begins at 8 a.m. with Bible study and prayer, followed by core subject instruction from 8:30 until 11:30. The next hour and a half are spent in meal preparation and clean up. The day ends at 4 p.m. after skill training. It is hoped that students will be able to use their training to start their own small businesses, making, for example, yeast rolls or sewing bags.

Vocational training manager Susan Kaminski is struck by the change that comes over these young women during their training:

When the girls come to our gate, eyes are downcast. They are emotionally and physically bruised, simply surviving. Most live in situations where they, as young girls, are used to [meeting] the needs of others, never experiencing the protection and nurture a child desires. Within months, these fragile young girls are transformed into vibrant, hopeful young women, anticipating the future God has prepared for them.

The success of the girls' centers, renamed Vocational Arts Programs in 2006, led to plans to develop similar centers for boys. The first Rafiki Boys' Center was opened in Nigeria in 2005.

Light in the Kitchen. Dingase washes up after a meal at the Rafiki Girls' Center in Malawi. During a nutrition class on the importance of a well-balanced diet, she asked if her health had been harmed when, at age ten, she lived in an orchard and had nothing to eat but mangoes for three months. Today Dingase works as an assistant mother in the village. (Tiffany R. C. Roach, 2003)

Friends. Two young girls talk outside a shop in Nigeria. (Lauren Elizabeth Thorp, 2004)

Alight. A pin-tailed whydah pauses to rest in Kenya. (Annie Jensen, 2005)

7

HOPE

Stories of Young Rafiki Girls

A tiny brick house perches on a steep hillside in Malawi. It is surrounded by banana trees and hand-hewn garden plots, and a clothesline is slung in front of the doorway. Inside are three connecting spaces—the first holds two rough chairs and a low table made from stalks of bamboo; the second is storage for a few pieces of clothing; the cement floor of the third is covered by two thin cloth sleeping pallets. A tiny shuttered window can be opened for light when the door is closed.

The cooking room is a completely bare space that can only be reached by walking outside the house. There, a small, round, metal container for wood, about a foot tall, sits near the open doorway and serves as a cooking fire. Around the side of the house is another empty room for bathing, and an outhouse is perched a few yards farther away. Water must be carried from a community tap at the bottom of the hill.

The four teenage girls who share this house, graduates of the RGC, consider themselves lucky. They provide food for themselves by sewing and selling quilts. The tiny church next door provided their home. Ethel, Etta, Maggie, and Sokwa sit on the front steps, arms wrapped around their knees, shy smiles on their faces, feet bare, to tell their stories.

Ethel watched her father die of AIDS when she was eight years old. She went to live with an aunt, who also died that year. Ethel was taken in by yet another aunt, who died when Ethel was fifteen, leaving her responsible for six younger cousins. All the family of her father died from diseases caused by AIDS. No one was left to help, so Ethel sold firewood to provide food for the children. Finally three of her cousins were married off, two were taken in by an orphanage, and

The Window. Etta leans against the small shuttered window of her house, listening as her friend Maggie is interviewed in Malawi. (Jenna M. Thorp, 2005)

41

Home. Maggie sits on the front steps of the house she shares with her three friends in Malawi. (Jenna M. Thorp, 2005)

another cousin was placed in a home, leaving Ethel alone in the house. Ethel's church put her in touch with Rafiki. The RGC had opened in October 2002, and there Ethel began vocational training. Soon afterward, her uncle came to the house and took away everything she had, including the suitcase in which she had been keeping her clothes. He chased her out of the house, saying she was not related to him by blood.

"In all these years I have been meeting difficulties in my life," Ethel says, "but I put my trust in [God]. I have been encouraged by many people to continue my three-year program at Rafiki, even though it was difficult to care for my cousins and myself, but God helped me a lot in so many things, both physical and spiritual. May all people who read this story be encouraged, and may they be honored, not by me, but God."

Nineteen-year-old Etta was born into a polygamous family in a village far from Mzuzu. Her father had three wives and nine children before the second wife died. Etta was born to the first wife.

"I have a father and mother," Etta says, "but I grew up in a miserable life." Her father wasn't working and couldn't afford to pay the school fees for his many children. Nor at times could he feed them. "In 1999 there was no food [in] the whole of Malawi," Etta continues. "I was eating nothing, and sometimes I was just drinking water. Some people were dying because of this famine, but I thank God I am still alive."

In 2002, Etta and a friend left for Mzuzu, hoping to find work. She had no relatives in town and begged to live with her friend's sister. Unable to find work for a year, she heard about Rafiki from another girl and began her training there in 2003. One month later, her friend's sister moved, leaving Etta to fend for herself.

"When I started living alone," she says, "I met many problems. . . . I started complaining and crying for school, and God gives me Rafiki, but no place to stay so that I can continue my education. I had no hope in my life. I was thinking that it is the end of my life."

Woodworker. A girl at the RGC in Malawi wields a chisel to carve letters into a wooden plank. (Tiffany R. C. Roach, 2003)

One of a Kind. Lydia is an orphan but full of laughter, with a reputation for sewing five times faster than her fellow students at the RGC in Nigeria. She hopes to become a tailor. Her teacher describes Lydia as "one of a kind." (Lauren Elizabeth Thorp, 2004)

When Etta stopped going to the Rafiki Girls' Center, the Brethren Church stepped in to provide the way for her to continue. She is determined to have a business of her own some day. "I want to make my future," she says. "I thank Madam Rosemary Jensen for the vision she had to open Rafiki Village in Africa. Indeed, she did a good job [for] those who are lacking [school] fees like me, and I thank all the people who are working together with her. It's not easy to do what you are doing. May God bless you all abundantly and protect you."

Maggie is the third oldest in a family with six children. Her father had four wives, of which her mother was the first. "My parents were Christian," she says, "and my dad became a Christian first, but because of many wives, he started to drink beer and many things. He started not to care for our family. . . . I know my mom was helping us to go to school by selling firewood. She was going to the bush and finding some wood to help."

In spite of her mother's help, Maggie had to leave secondary school. Her father developed cancer and died three years later in 2001. "I left school because my dad started to be sick, so I looked for help for my mom. She was busy caring for my dad with the money she found. . . . I came to my sister's in Mzuzu to look for help, but my brother-in-law said he didn't have school fees to pay for me. He was paying for his family and his brothers and sisters."

Her brother-in-law told her about Rafiki. Maggie says, "I started learning at Rafiki, and I was staying with my brother-in-law. . . . He was very harsh, and I was staying just because of school. I didn't want to leave Rafiki. He chased me, shouting, 'I don't want you to stay here because I am not working! I do not have anything to care for you, including food.' But he was giving [me] food. I ran at first and [then] walked home but I was thinking about school."

Maggie knew that her mother was too poor to support her. She tried once more to stay with her brother-in-law, but soon was able to move in with her friends Etta, Ethel, and Sokwa. She hopes her training at Rafiki will help her to become independent and to help others. "I was nothing," she says, "but now I am something. . . . I know that God has a purpose for me."

Lunch. The girls learn to make a meal at the RGC in Nigeria. (Lauren Elizabeth Thorp, 2004)

Blessings. Etta, Ethel, and Maggie reflect after sharing their stories outside their home in Malawi. (Jenna M. Thorp, 2005)

The oldest of five children, Sokwa's parents died when she was ten. Her step-sister brought her to Mzuzu, where she finished primary school, but her step-sister lacked the funds for her to attend secondary school. Sokwa began training at the Rafiki Girls' Center. A short time later, her step-sister married. As Sokwa returned home from school one day, she was met by her step-sister and brother-in-law.

"My step-sister said, 'From today I don't want you to be at my house because now you are old enough, and you cannot stay with me again.' Then she threw my clothes outside. I stayed outside from 5 p.m. up to midnight, then she said

Agnes. Agnes pauses on her way to class at the Kenya RGC. (Annie Jensen, 2005)

I could enter, but tomorrow I should know where to go. It was very difficult for me. Imagine, I did not have any relatives in Mzuzu. The next day in the morning I went to my home village, but I was not feeling well. I was crying each and every day."

Once again the church stepped in, enabling Sokwa to continue at Rafiki. Soon after her return, she heard her step-sister's son was ill, and went to visit him.

"While I was still on the way, I met my brother-in-law. He started shouting and beating me up to my step-sister's house." Sokwa tried to leave, but her step-sister and brother-in-law followed her and dragged her back to their house. "They said I was not safe where I am staying because they were thinking that maybe boys are coming to our house because we are staying with girls only. They took me and put me in the room because they were thinking that I can run."

The pastor of Sokwa's church heard what happened and the next day came searching for her. "He found me," she says, "with my head and face covered with a cloth by my step-sister." Sokwa was returned to the little house. "I thank God for you people, and Rosemary for deciding to open this school here in Malawi. May God bless you for your love to us."

All across Africa, the stories are similar. In Kenya, two more graduates of RGC wait quietly to share their stories outside the Rafiki Girls' Center. Their faces are scrubbed, and they are neatly attired in the burgundy and navy Rafiki uniforms. Their smiles come easily, and they are not afraid to look others in the eye.

Faith is one of the younger children in a family of seven. Her parents died when she was fourteen, and Faith moved to Nairobi. "I was living with my cousin, and the husband of my cousin wanted me to get married. . . . They were thinking because I am parentless, they can just get the money to get married. And then I refused. When I refused, they chased me away."

Faith went to stay with her brother. "When I went there," she says, "my life got worse and worse. He was married, and you know how life is; my sister-in-law was not nice, and my brother was not nice. They got drunk, and sometimes when I came out from school and went back there, the door [was] locked. I [had to] stay outside."

She left for a friend's house, and then went to stay with a woman who was unrelated to her. Although Faith stayed with her for some time, the woman eventually turned her out. "She told me that blood is thicker than water. It was painful for me. I started even questioning God. Why is this happening to me for sure if you really love me? Am I the one who told my parents to die so that I can suffer? But from there I saw God's hand because God opened a way."

Faith found Rafiki through her church and went back to live with her brother, who by then was employed. At age nineteen, she looks forward to graduation. She is also praying that God will provide work and a house: "I need a big house because I want to help these people. Like yesterday there was one of the ladies who was being beaten by her brother. She talked a lot, and when I was comparing her life with my life, I was thinking this was the same thing I was going through. And I spoke to this lady and comforted her, and now we are friends. . . . I don't know where God will put me, but I want to help."

At twenty-one, Agnes is from a single-parent home in a small village. She also could not continue her education because of school fees. "And when I trusted God for that," she says, "He did do something, because He created a way for me to come to Rafiki." She is now completing her last semester.

"The people I live with are not my parents. They are not my relatives. But she's my godmother, and she's kind to me, because she offered herself to accommodate me and provide all my needs." Her godmother does not live near the center, and Agnes must use public transportation to get there every morning, a journey of an hour and a half each way. "God has been faithful to me," she says, "because the transport has been paid for. When I come here in the center, I am kind of comforted, because where I live is not that comforting. But at least my hopes are kind of resurrected."

Agnes would like to continue her education, and possibly take a course in hotel management.

Sing. Etta, Sarah, and Esther sing along with the rest of the class during the Malawi Rafiki Village dedication ceremony held in a tent. (Annie Jensen, 2005)

Loom. One of the looms used by the girls at the RGC in Uganda.
(Annie Jensen, 2005)

"Yeah. I hope God will create still [for] me a way for achieving all that."

A few months after she said these things, Agnes graduated from the Rafiki Girls' Center and gave the following graduation speech:

I greet you all in the name of our Lord Jesus Christ. Good afternoon. I would like to welcome you all to today's ceremony and also thank each one of you who have come to share the joy of our three years' harvest with us. I am also grateful for this opportunity as a student spokesperson, to address you. I regard it an honor, to stand in front of you. As all of you can see, there are five of us who are distinct from others. The reason is that, theoretically and practically, we have come to an end of what we have been learning in Rafiki, though it is not an end of education. There is still a part remaining to be done, and that is to implement and have experience in things we have learned here.

Briefly, I would like to say what Rafiki Girls' Center does. It admits girls and offers them courses, which will be great help for them in the present and in the future. It resurrects their dreams and gives them hope for the bright future. The most significant lessons we have undertaken here are about God. As a matter of fact, we have matured spiritually much more than when we first joined, and our mortal man is reinforced. And also we can face the future without any terror. For me, I had given up with life but when I joined Rafiki, a new page was flipped.

I came to know that I have the potential to better my life and be a helpful person in the society. And I hope it is the same thing with my fellow students. Therefore we have taken very crucial courses, which are of much help now and later in the future. Some of the courses that we have undertaken are computer, catering, tailoring, and many others. We have been here for three years, and we have all reasons to thank God. May all praises and glory be returned unto Him for His preservation and care that He has taken upon us.

My thanks goes to Rosemary Jensen for her dream to start centers in Africa which cared for girls and less fortunate children in the communities, and also to those who worked with her to implement the dream. I cannot forget our wonderful teachers who have really sacrificed their time and energy to serve us.

Last but not least I want to thank my fellow students for the encouragement I have gotten from them. And any other person who participated in any way, receives my measureless thanks, and may the Lord God bless you abundantly.

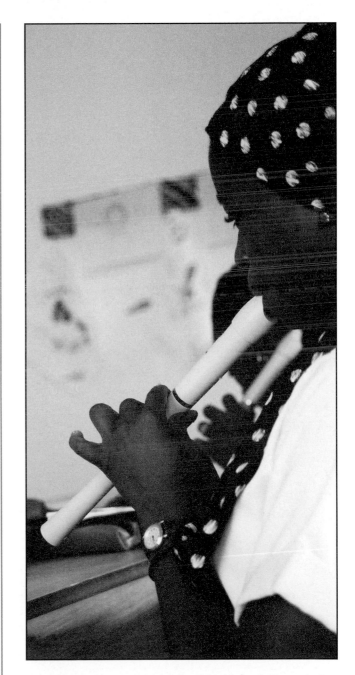

Sewing. A girl learns to sew at the RGC in Tanzania, using a foot-powered sewing machine. (Tiffany R. C. Roach, 2003)

Music. Sarah concentrates as she plays the recorder during music class at the Nigeria RGC. (Lauren Elizabeth Thorp, 2004)

Just Part of the Herd. A family of zebras in Ngorongoro Crater in Tanzania. (Annie Jensen, 2005)

8

A WHOLE VILLAGE

How the Rafiki Village Developed

A man named Professor Egbert Chibambo called Rosemary Jensen one Christmas from Seattle, Washington. It was the year 2001, and while visiting his brother, Egbert became intrigued by what the Rafiki Foundation was doing in Africa. He introduced himself as the mayor of Mzuzu, a city of one hundred twenty thousand in northern Malawi, and he was very direct. Could Rafiki come to Mzuzu and build an orphanage?

Rosemary said no. Rafiki had been building in the national capital cities. If there was to be an orphanage in Malawi, it would be built in Lilongwe. Egbert was undaunted. There are nine thousand orphans in Mzuzu alone, he countered, and before their conversation ended, he persuaded Rosemary to come and see for herself.

Two months later, Rosemary and her team arrived in Mzuzu. Egbert arranged a grand tour of the city, including hospitals, churches, and businesses. There were no orphanages, so Egbert had instructed the orphans to gather at schools. As the day wore on, rain began to fall, the group fell behind schedule and pulled onto the grounds of one school an hour and a half late. Yet standing there silently in the pouring rain, waiting to receive them, were nearly eight hundred orphans. Never before had Rosemary seen so many children in one place without mother or father, dependent on an impoverished community for their very existence.

When the team went to officially register Rafiki in Malawi, one of the cabinet ministers, after hearing about the Rafiki concept of meeting the needs of the whole child, told Rosemary that the work she was doing was very good. Then he challenged her to build a model that others could emulate. The Malawi government offered the Rafiki Foundation 185 acres of land.

Before the Plaster. A view into the Rafiki Girls' Center in Mzuzu, Malawi, prior to plastering. (Christopher A. Moyer, 2004)

Mixing Concrete. Workers mix concrete for the Rafiki Girls' Center in Accra, Ghana. (Christopher A. Moyer, 2004)

Rosemary was astounded. Rafiki only required thirty acres for a children's center. Flying toward home, Rosemary wondered why Rafiki had been offered so much land. "With that much land, I could build a whole village!" she mused. The idea was born. Rafiki took only seventy-five acres, but they had a new goal—to build a model Rafiki Village that others could copy.

The village model was a natural progression for Rafiki. More extensive facilities had already begun to evolve, particularly in Ghana. The Rafiki Village program as now conceived was developed around four kinds of facilities: (1) the RCC cottages for children; (2) staff housing; (3) training centers for girls and boys; and (4) a multipurpose gathering place. Although the village concept was born in Malawi, the prototype was constructed in Ghana, beginning with the Rafiki Children's Center.

Chris Moyer explains that the types of available building materials vary quite a bit from country to country, so each planning and construction project must be planned and carried out according to what is available. Quality, though, is always stressed in Rafiki building projects, says Richard Walenta. "The quality that we're demanding from our contractors is different than they're used to. It's not that they're not capable of doing the work, it's just that they're not used to that standard."

Currently there are Rafiki Villages in Ghana, Nigeria, Uganda, Kenya, and Malawi. Each consists of homes and schools for 160 orphan children, employment preparation schools for sixty teenage girls and sixty teenage boys, staff housing, a hall for performances and sports, and a medical clinic, which provides quarterly medical care for the community.

Each Rafiki village is managed by an on-site director. An example is Yeen Lan Lam, who at this writing is village director and volunteer coordinator in Nairobi. She was a Bible Study Fellowship (BSF) discussion leader in Singapore, where she met Rosemary Jensen and was sold on the Rafiki vision. After years of working in Nairobi, Yeen Lan Lam finds that every day still poses its own challenges. "They could be anything from not having water or power to the treacherous roads that we have to struggle with—but the joys often more than overcome some of the challenges."

Jos Village. The entrance gate and buildings of the Nigeria Rafiki Village, as seen from the Rafiki Boys' Center site across the street. (Christopher A. Moyer, 2004)

According to Yeen Lan Lam, the community health clinics go beyond physical healing to spiritual and emotional support for the people. "The results speak for themselves," she says, "when you have people coming as early as three in the morning, [lining up] in the rain for a clinic that opens at eight o'clock—that means a lot for me. And for the team of doctors to work nonstop until eight or nine o'clock [at night]—that is very significant."

Each children's area is divided into eighteen, ten-child cottages. An accredited school is available for pre-kindergarten through grade twelve. Also available are dining facilities, a playing field, an infirmary, and agricultural land. Rafiki makes provision for short-term programs three times a year during holidays. These enrichment programs are called GAMES, an acronym for

Bicycle. A boy and his bicycle, a popular means of conveyance in Tanzania. (Annie Jensen, 2005)

Celebration. Rosemary celebrates the dedication of the Rafiki Village in Nigeria with local musicians. (Lauren Elizabeth Thorp, 2004)

G: Games, such as chess, puzzles, and checkers;
A: Arts, including painting, drawing, dance, drama, and crafts;
M: Music, both choir and instrumental;
E: Enrichment, including field trips to zoos and museums, explorations in how things work, practical skills like planting a garden, and occasions for learning social skills and manners; and
S: Sports, such as gymnastics, soccer, volleyball, and kite flying.

While regular teachers take a much-needed break, these vacation schools are organized by one of the ROS with help from short-term mission teachers. Rafiki

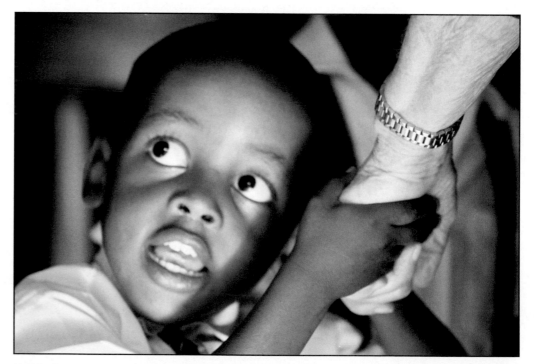

Hold On. Brian holds on to Rosemary's hand with both of his during her visit to the Rafiki Village in Nairobi, Kenya. (Annie Jensen, 2005)

hopes eventually to open these vacation schools to enrich the lives of other children in the surrounding community.

"I look at the little ones," Bob Jensen says. "Some of them came in so scrawny you can hardly believe. Some were left in toilets, some were left at the gate with their umbilical cord still damp and dangling. And to see them—one, two, three years later—running around and playing, so joyful. And they have a village. They may not know who their parents are, but they have a village. They have friends."

"Here we are in the middle of the African continent," Chris says, "doing entire villages all over the place. I mean that's an unbelievable opportunity. I have to kind of pinch myself once in awhile when I realize I've been given that chance."

Joy. Elube Sichinga, bathed in the golden light of the tent, leads the local church chorus in song and dance in the Malawi Rafiki Village dedication ceremony. (Annie Jensen, 2005)

Formwork. A column form for the Rafiki Girls' Center in Accra, Ghana. (Christopher A. Moyer, 2004)

Open Door. Two girls and a baby enter an open gate in Nigeria. (Lauren Elizabeth Thorp, 2004)

9

COMING ALONGSIDE

Rafiki Overseas Staff and Volunteers

Today a number of North American churches and educational institutions want to work in partnership with the Rafiki Foundation. Through programs like Rafiki Orphan Sponsors, Rafiki Partner Churches, and Rafiki Prayer Groups, there are many ways to come alongside the people of Africa, but perhaps none is as vital as those who give of themselves by signing on as long- and short-term missionaries.

Long-term workers are collectively called the Rafiki Overseas Staff (ROS). It takes seven qualified ROS to operate a RCC; RGCs and RBCs each require four. The kind of people who become part of the ROS are chosen for

- hearts that are full of God's love and willing to sacrifice in service to others;
- their understanding of God's word and readiness to live by it;
- their willingness to devote a lifetime to service;
- their physical and emotional ability to do the work, leaving behind attachment to home, family, and job; and
- their appreciation for and submission to the Rafiki Foundation program.

It takes twenty qualified ROS, working alongside eighty nationals, to build and operate a village. As the complexity of such an organization became evident, Rosemary Jensen quickly saw the importance of capable, experienced village directors.

One such director is Ken Dulany, who left behind a twenty-year career in banking. He and his wife moved to the village in Ghana in 2003, where he

Burden. Beasts of burden patiently carry their loads in Ethiopia. (Annie Jensen, 2005)

became the volunteer coordinator. He then moved to Ethiopia as director for a new work there.

"We had a great two years in Ghana. The best part of Ghana was the people . . . the closest thing to African Texans." Once when his wife's car wound up in a roadside ditch, sixteen people jumped in to lift the car back onto the road. "It's a hot place, but we've acclimated. It's become home."

While in Ghana, Ken faithfully sent in monthly reports. His ability to communicate effectively in the reports was one reason he was picked to be the new village director. "One of the things we found out," he laughs, "was that Rosemary reads those things!" As village director for the Ethiopia Rafiki Village project, Ken will oversee its construction, while attempting to absorb the customs and languages of a culture quite different from that in Ghana.

A great many tasks are filled by the ROS, each team with its own unique flavor and responsibilities. In Nigeria, Children's Center director Jackie Anderson sent the following account about a trip to visit children orphaned in the Muslim-Christian violence in 2004. That journey to the village of Tunkus included a team of a doctor, a state social worker, and a man who works with Christians who are former Muslims, and who are targeted by those in Islam and excluded from churches because of fear.

> The rough road took us through the outskirts of Yelwa, where the Christians have relocated. In town it is apparent which homes belonged formerly to Christians as they were in various stages of destruction. Not a roof on one, and many nearly flattened. . . .
>
> As we slowly drove, jaw wide opened and wet-eyed, we stopped at a church. This is where the riot started February 24, 2004. The Muslims surrounded the church and entered with machete and fire, killing most. Those who ran outside were quickly killed also. We soberly walked the property and viewed the devastation—rolled over and burned cars, two roofless buildings, and the altar area where stood a simple podium that has been fabricated to meet the needs of the few who are continuing to meet together

Worn. Ruins across from the Rafiki Village in Nigeria. (Lauren Elizabeth Thorp, 2004)

Blue Africa. The view during the descent into Ngorongoro Crater in Tanzania. (Annie Jensen, 2005)

to worship and pray. On that podium raised area were said to have been many dead bodies. The grave site outside beyond the tall corn stalks we walked through contains seventy bodies in a mass grave. That was the beginning of crisis that was reported eventually even to the USA in early May 2004. The blame was placed on the Christians, as they advanced a reprisal which continued the killing into March and April. . . .

We drove on another forty kilometers toward Tunkus. The conversation in the car all the way was challenging. . . . I heard repeatedly (although I was graciously welcomed) a certain disdain for the westerners and their ignorance. Even as my thoughts stopped me, soon too, a broad and fairly deep river came which separated our vehicle from the village where a group of orphans

The Kid. A young girl and her goat along a dusty road in the Ethiopian countryside. (Annie Jensen, 2005)

The Face of Hope. The youngest girl to attend the Rafiki Girls' Center in Moshi, Lindaeli looks across the cornfield near her home in Tanzania. (Annie Jensen, 2005)

waited for us to interview and screen. Mark in his boldness didn't allow the barrier to deter us. . . . We all exited the Jeep and crossed on a narrow foot bridge—if you could call it that. A large group of boys were gathered, assisting transport of goods from one side to the other. Mark had them enter the river and mark out the shallowest place to pass. When the car died in the middle, they pushed, and he made it through. The water had even entered the door jambs! We thanked God and quickly returned on route. Just a few kilometers and we were there.

The children were free and ready. Maybe thirty were there but not all for us to see, as most were older. They are being cared for by a local pastor/church planter there. When the trouble came to Yelwa, some women quickly took the children over the river-obstructed road to a place of safety. Some of these children have a parent remaining. Some have no idea [if a parent is alive], and some are sure of [their parents'] death. It is those ones who could validate both parents deceased (one of the four-year-old boys told the social worker how his mommy and daddy were killed, as though he had been a witness). Because some have siblings who are older and others are not sure of the status of parents, we were able to consider only three: Bistu, a four-ish-year-old boy, Fotkum, also about four, and Kefas, one year, two months. . . .

After such a day, the photos are clear in my mind: the beauty of the green rainy season landscape, blue sky with billowy clouds, rural Africa—naked people bathing and laundering in swollen rivers, prominent vistas of a broad panorama. . . . So we pray. . . . The prayer is earnest, and the work is plenty. One child. One life. One future. One hope. One Lord. One Faith. Grateful that we know how it all ends. Challenged to be so tenacious in my stand. Privileged to have these words to share with you so that you can see. So you, too, can stand with us in your place.

The three children identified by Jackie were accepted into the Rafiki Village in Jos, Nigeria, in December 2004.

The ROS are aided by short-term volunteers, age eighteen and older, who travel to Africa at their own expense for one to four weeks. One such volunteer, Tyler Anderson, a physician's assistant, describes his trip:

Where do I begin? How can I share with you what it was like to spend two weeks as a member of a medical team at the Rafiki Village outside Nairobi, Kenya? I honestly do not recall the hours spent in planes and airports, nor do I remember the landscape and animals so much as the faces, smiles, and eyes. Revelation 21:4 says, "He will wipe every tear from their eyes. There will be no more death or mourning or crying or pain, for the old order of things has passed away."

The Lord has laid on my heart a deep desire to help dry those tears in any way I can. Having been to Africa I will never be the same. I can't be. There are nearly two million orphans in Kenya, and the same number of adults and children living with HIV. More than 57 percent of Kenya's population lives in poverty. God has my attention, and I cannot turn away.

Joy and heartache overwhelmed me every day I was there and continue to echo in me even now. I looked into eyes filled with tears: a twenty-five-year-old married mother of two who heard, from my lips, a death sentence in the form of a positive HIV test. An eighty-two-year-old man who was slowly starving to death because he had no teeth, no money, no strength to work, no social security check, no food bank to visit. Many of my days were spent with a lump in my throat and tears welling up in my own eyes.

But there was also unspeakable joy and evidence that some tears are being wiped away. Sharing a meal and playing with four-year-old boys named Onesimus and Moses warmed my

Blue Sky. The late afternoon sky over Ngorongoro Crater in Tanzania. (Jenna M. Thorp, 2005)

Scaffold. Concrete workers perch on scaffolding made from eucalyptus trees in Ethiopia. (Annie Jensen, 2005)

heart as their eyes gleamed and smiles shone bright. They were at peace, loved, and at home. These two are no longer orphans, having been adopted into their new Rafiki family. They have a national mother who cares for them in a cottage within the village. Even more remarkable was seeing the faith, confidence, and hope radiate from the eyes of teenage girls who are students in Rafiki's three-year vocational training center. . . .

I want to go back. I would get on a plane right now if I could.

Moshi Children. Curious children gather along the roadside in the town of Moshi, Tanzania. (Tiffany R. C. Roach, 2003)

Market. An open-air market brimming with colorful produce in Nigeria. (Lauren Elizabeth Thorp, 2004)

Letters. A post office in Nigeria. (Lauren Elizabeth Thorp, 2004)

10

WHOOPS, JUMPS, AND TEARS OF JOY

The Heart of a Donor

In one of the peculiar reverses of the Christian life, the more we give up, the more we gain.

—Rosemary Jensen

The Rafiki Foundation would not exist without the support of generous gifts, most from people who prefer to give without recognition. Many sponsor individual children for $100 a month, or teenagers in vocational training. Others provide funds for construction and maintenance, operational expenses, staff, or administration. Some donate gifts large enough to have a major impact on the work. Not long ago, a few such donors traveled to Africa to see the work, and one married couple talked about their impressions:

> I've known about Rafiki since its inception. I've always been touched by the possibility of helping others. I know God has been very good to us and it seemed appropriate to share our many blessings with the Rafiki Foundation.
>
> I've been blessed by God. At some point you have to think about why you've got these things. It just seemed the right thing to do. I thought the [Rafiki] concept made a lot of sense. So we're here.
>
> I'd sent an e-mail saying what we were going to do, and how much we'd like to give. I think there were a fair amount of whoops,

The Path. A pathway leading from the gazebo and playground to the community buildings at the Kenya Rafiki Village. (Jenna M. Thorp, 2005)

View from the Top. The top of the gate to Rafiki Village in Nairobi, Kenya. (Annie Jensen, 2005)

jumps, and tears of joy. [Rosemary] called to thank [us] for the gift, and she said, "I'd really like you to come along and see what Rafiki [is] actually doing." I thought it would be an amazing experience. I had always been afraid to go to Africa, but I thought there is no better person to go with than Rosemary.

This is the first time we've been to Africa. I've always wanted to come. Always tried to talk [my wife] into coming, always been unsuccessful. Along comes Rafiki, and [she] says, "We're going to Africa." We've seen a number of countries now—all unique. The poverty is pretty obvious. The people seem happy. You can tell by the housing that they are productive. It's very hard to put into words how you feel about this. You get sensory overload.

I was hesitant about coming to Africa. I was afraid it was too remote. I wasn't sure what I'd find. I have to say I've been pleasantly surprised in some ways, and it has been a fabulous experience. It certainly opened my eyes.

I found the countries to be absolutely beautiful for the most part. I found the people to be open and friendly. . . . You look in their faces, and you can almost look into their hearts, particularly with the girls who are in the Rafiki villages. Their hearts and faces are open, just reflecting how God has worked in their hearts. . . . In driving through Nairobi and seeing the people and the poverty and the need of children, when we got to the Rafiki Village I was frankly amazed at the transformation of what we saw outside the gate and what was inside the gate. Clearly God had changed the lives of the children who were fortunate enough to be in the Rafiki Village. And I see the same thing here in Uganda. The girls [in the RGC] in Tanzania look you right in the eye. Their hands are out to shake your hand. They openly are embracing the world, where had they been left outside the gate, they would not be able to do that.

[The children of Africa] are very happy, and they have nothing. There is a genuineness and positive feeling. But then what happens to them? Reality sets in. So to me that's the best thing about Rafiki. You take that wonderful, positive, almost innocent feeling about the world and keep it through God. You don't let it go away.

I think the one thing I see with the Rafiki kids is the promise. They have a promise and a future. . . . And I feel very privileged to be part of this, part of them, seeing this at the very inception, seeing just what one person, one idea, can actually do, seeing how God works change, how it grows. . . . I think you can't come away from an experience like this without having a change in how you approach the world. We've seen so many things different from the way we live, we probably will have a higher view of God and His workings. We'll start with that.

When I pray, I thank God for His blessings. Sometimes the problems seem to be so impossible that where do you start? To see a systematic, well-thought-out approach—it restores your faith. It's so good to see people doing things that have an impact, rather than just complain about the seeming overwhelming nature of it.

There's a lot of talk about coming alongside, and that's what Rafiki does.

Two of this couple's children accompanied them on their trip, and their twenty-year-old son was also interviewed. His surprise at the enormity of Africa, at the pride and resilience of the people, and his pleasure in a whole different culture are reflected in excerpts from his comments:

Slice of Life. The view from a hillside of some of the homes in Ghana. (Lauren Elizabeth Thorp, 2004)

Nairobi. A jumble of buildings alongside a road in Nairobi, Kenya. (Annie Jensen, 2005)

It's definitely been a revelation of sorts—a big culture shock. Everything in Africa is much bigger. It's kind of strange. . . . The centers are beautiful. They're really well-built. The construction is great. The kids are really friendly. The way they carry themselves is remarkable. The [Malawi] dedication was pretty extreme. It wasn't like anything I've ever seen before, and the people I was with—being such a big part of it. It was marvelous—very eye-opening.

The way people can come out here for years on end and have the dedication to help these people they've never met before—to help them become young adults and get on with their lives—it's really amazing. It really touched me. It's opened my eyes and broadened my horizons to what there is in life.

Hay. An elderly man strolls past a haystack in rural Ethiopia. (Annie Jensen, 2005)

Crater. The white clouds above Ngorongoro Crater are reflected in a meandering stream in Tanzania. (Jenna M. Thorp, 2005)

Bird's Eye. An eagle soars above the clouds in Tanzania. (Annie Jensen, 2005)

11
A BIGGER VISION

The Future of Rafiki

With model villages established or well underway in ten African nations, it was only a matter of time before the concept attracted enough attention to be replicated. Another donor stepped forward to provide funds to build a smaller version of these villages—one in each of the ten nations—at a cost of $1.25 million each.

His concept was the start of the Satellite Program.

Churches of various denominations had already worked with the Foundation to provide church homes for the Rafiki children, and to help with the quarterly community medical clinics. With the inception of the Satellite Program, Rafiki helps establish satellites that are staffed by people chosen by the local church. To operate a "satellite village," an African congregation works in partnership with a North American congregation. Each satellite consists of an orphanage for one hundred children, two schools, a RGC, a RBC, and staff housing. The first satellite village was placed in Umbra Rimi, Nigeria, and the idea spread from there. As of this writing, four satellite villages are under construction.

Along the coast in Winneba, Ghana, young boys try to make a living by untangling fishnets underwater. These boys are virtual slaves, and many drown, neither mourned nor cared for. The Rafiki partner church in this particular area, concerned about these boys, approached a tribal leader. The chief recognized in the satellite a great benefit for the people in his community and donated twenty acres to the church.

It would cost $250 million to build and operate one hundred satellite villages for five years. The goal of the Rafiki Foundation is to plant ten satellites in each of the ten countries where they have a presence. Looking beyond this first stage is an even larger dream that, as funds become available, as many as ten

Lady in Blue. A woman heads toward the town marketplace with her wares perched safely on her head, balanced by the positioning of her head scarf in Nigeria. (Lauren Elizabeth Thorp, 2004)

Sunrise. The sun rising over Ngorongoro Crater, Tanzania, dispelling the lingering mist. (Annie Jensen, 2005)

satellite homes for widows with children could be established around each of the villages.

The numbers are staggering and the potential impact on these African countries can only be imagined. Reaching these goals will require an immense effort, but Rosemary Jensen speaks with certainty for those who are looking ahead when she describes their shared motivation, God's love for them: "What drives me is really the love of God. I am constrained to do this work. I think this is what I was born for. It's what I was made to do. Beyond that, the needs of the people, they grab me every time I come to Africa."

"If you were to ask me ten years ago if we would have Rafiki Villages," John Chun says, "I never would have believed it. I suspect we will have many satellite villages in at least ten countries. We are all part of the same work. The people here are just beautiful. The relationships we have made with the people of Africa are indescribable. It changes your life. It changes you."

According to Bob Jensen, "The thing that stands out the most are the children who have come in to the Rafiki fold and have looked out and said, 'I am so lucky to be here.'" He adds, explaining the importance of a broader vision, "[They] have expressed, as they have grown, a desire to help others."

Mike Yeats assists the Rafiki Foundation with investment. He's enthusiastic about the satellite concept, and expresses his confidence about Rafiki's role in reducing poverty and increasing the level of education in Africa:

> I'm awfully excited about where Rafiki is going. . . . As far as Africa is concerned, I'm awfully optimistic because I think programs have a tendency to move laterally for a long period of time, then things begin to happen—such as the internet, such as technology, such as revolution in many forms—and all of a sudden you have a climb in standard of living, a climb in broader educational base. You can feel we're getting awfully close. I think Rafiki is playing a role in that. This Satellite Program could be just the leverage that none of us anticipated several years ago.

But Rosemary, who calls herself an American African, believes their role could have impact far beyond their imagination. "I love Africa," she says. "I have a heart for these people. Even when we are not here, my heart is in Africa. But I must admit we had a much smaller vision than we do now. God is concerned about the needs of the helpless. . . . Whole nations could be changed. I believe if you could change ten nations in Africa, you could change the continent."

Rwanda. A cityscape in the capital of Rwanda. (Annie Jensen, 2005)

Village Girl. A young girl watches shyly from behind a makeshift hedge of thorn branches outside a village in Tanzania. (Tiffany R. C. Roach, 2003)

Transport. A bus park in Addis Ababa, Ethiopia. (Annie Jensen, 2005)

GETTING THERE

All the Details

HOME OFFICE

The Rafiki Foundation home office is in San Antonio, Texas. Twelve full-time and a number of part-time staff and volunteers handle administrative and financial management. The foundation can be contacted at

The Rafiki Foundation, Inc.
P.O. Box 1988
Eustis, FL 32727
E-mail: rafiki@rafiki-foundation.org
Web site: www.rafiki-foundation.org

The Rafiki Foundation also maintains a branch office in Nairobi, Kenya, providing administrative support for the villages.

RAFIKI'S PLAN FOR AFRICA

Rafiki sends out qualified professionals to work with nationals in Africa to achieve the following goals:

PHYSICAL

- Keep orphans and vulnerable children (OVC) alive and healthy
- Instruct OVC in good lifetime health habits
- Instruct OVC and selected adults in maintaining an HIV/AIDS-free community

Chris. Photographer Christopher A. Moyer makes notes about a land site being considered by Rafiki for a village in Ethiopia. (Annie Jensen, 2005)

Tiffany. Photographer Tiffany R. C. Roach awash in children outside the Rafiki Girls' Center in Malawi. (Bob Jensen, 2003)

SPIRITUAL

- Bring OVC into a knowledge of God and His Son the Lord Jesus Christ
- Teach OVC the principles of godly living as outlined in Scripture
- Provide opportunities for OVC to serve God by serving others

EDUCATIONAL

- Give orphans a classical Christian education from preschool through primary school (grade 6)
- Give orphans opportunities for a quality secondary school education
- Give limited academic and vocational training to vulnerable teenagers

Jenna and Ryan. Photographers Jenna M. Thorp and Ryan Spencer at work in Ethiopia. (Annie Jensen, 2005)

SOCIAL

- Instruct OVC on the rights and responsibilities of being a citizen in their countries
- Help OVC to operate in an international setting
- Educate OVC in the history and cultural ways of their countries

OUTREACH

- Serve as a training resource for churches and other groups that might want to replicate Rafiki's ministry
- Serve the community by providing specific types of health care

Lauren. Photographer Lauren Elizabeth Thorp surrounded by children at the Rafiki Village in Nigeria. (Rosemary Jensen, 2004)

STRATEGY

Rafiki's strategy in achieving these goals is to:

1. Establish one Rafiki Training Village in each country that will be directly operated and staffed by the Rafiki Foundation, Inc.

2. Establish ten Rafiki Satellite Villages in each country that will receive training, support, and supervision through the Rafiki Training Village.

3. Establish ten Rafiki Satellite Homes around each satellite village and around each Rafiki Training Village. The satellite village or Rafiki Training Village will provide training, support, and supervision to the satellite homes.

ACCOUNTABILITY

The Rafiki Foundation's board of directors consists of nine members committed to the vision and mission of the Rafiki Foundation. The organization is a member of the Evangelical Council for Financial Accountability. The stringent rules and oversight of this organization are important in that those who give funds can do so with confidence that money will go to the purpose that the donor designates.

RAFIKI EXCHANGE

The Rafiki Exchange sells handmade items created at the Rafiki Girls' Centers, including jewelry, textiles, wood carving, and specialty items unique to the culture of origin. The exchange is located in San Antonio by the home office and operates as a retail outlet, with sales by telephone and Web site as well. All money from the sale of these products goes to support the girls' centers. The exchange and its telephone number at 210-244-2601 is open Monday through Friday afternoons, San Antonio time.

MINIMISSIONS

Rafiki calls its short-term impact missions "MiniMissions." Applications can be obtained by writing or calling the home office. Training is provided in San Antonio for volunteers interested in going on a MiniMission. The home office works with each volunteer in choosing the best assignment and timing for a trip, as well as to coordinate travel plans and help with required documentation.

While in Africa, volunteers stay in the guest house at the village. Short-term workers assist by doing such things as

- using prepared lesson plans to teach classes;
- encouraging the girls during skill training;
- helping prepare lunch;
- reading stories to children and helping at bedtime;

A Moment. Author and photographer Annie Jensen takes a break outside a government building while city officials discuss property acquisition with Rafiki members in Ethiopia. (Ryan Spencer, 2005)

Love. Bob and Rosemary Jensen walk to dinner in the rain at Rafiki Village, Nigeria. (Lauren Elizabeth Thorp, 2004)

- providing activities during free time after school;
- providing an adult presence in the dining room;
- being a teacher's helper during school;
- assisting in the medical clinic; and
- helping with the GAMES program during school breaks.

PRAYER GROUPS

Those interested in this work are encouraged to form or join a Rafiki Prayer Group (RPG). RPGs are registered. Information on starting a registered group or finding an existing group can be obtained by calling 210-244-2600 or by e-mail at rafiki@rafiki-foundation.org. General information about the prayer program is on the Web at rpg@rafiki-foundation.org.

RPGs support Rafiki through prayer for villages, staff, and programs. Along with prayer, groups can help by promoting the sale of Rafiki products; going on, or encouraging others to participate in, a short-term mission trip; giving to sponsor children or other needs in the organization.

PARTNER CHURCHES

Local congregations can also call the San Antonio home office to take part in a church partnership. Church partners can help by including the organization in their missions budget, adopting a village as a church project, sending out short-term or long-term workers, and by prayer and telling others of the work. Rafiki can help the church send short-term and long-term missionaries. Rafiki missionaries are available to come to speak at a church and provide updates and letters on their work.